The Steam Hammer Man

James Nasmyth (1808 - 1890)

Author: John Aldred

Contents

		Page number
Foreword		2
Chapter 1	The young James	4
Chapter 2	James in London	10
Chapter 3	After Henry Maudslay	16
Chapter 4	James Nasmyth at Patricroft	20
Chapter 5	James Nasmyth and the Steam Hammer	34
Chapter 6	Business expands	40
Chapter 7	Pastimes and hobbies	46
Chapter 8	Retirement	50
Chapter 9	Conclusion	56
Chapter 10	References and further reading	60

JOHN ALDRED was born in Fleetwood on the Fylde coast. After University and National Service in the Royal Air Force, he taught at a Grammar School near Liverpool. He moved to Worsley in 1963 and joined the staff at Worsley Wardley Grammar School. In 1972 he moved to Eccles College in charge of Geography. Since his retirement, he has developed an early interest in history and now spends his time lecturing and writing about the history of the Worsley area. His books include *"Worsley - an Historical Geography"*, *"Worsley in 1807"* and a number of monographs on local topics.

Foreword

James Nasmyth Portrait

The publication of John Aldred's account of James Nasmyth coincides with the approach of the bi-centenary of this great engineer's birth.

The 150th anniversary, in 1958, was marked in Eccles by the establishment of a special collection of Nasmyth records held at what was then Eccles Public Library, the publication of a catalogue of this collection and the holding of a Nasmyth Exhibition. Since that time our knowledge of Nasmyth has considerably advanced in the wake of further additions to the archive, new research and publications. It is therefore to be

"*John Aldred has successfully captured the essential quality of the man*"...

applauded that John Aldred has sifted through much of the new material to produce this highly readable, cogent and lucid summary of James Nasmyth's life and work. For those who wish to delve deeper, he has included a number of suggestions for further reading.

If he had been born in the fifteenth, instead of the nineteenth, century Nasmyth would have been hailed as a Renaissance Man. His interests and achievements extended well beyond money-making and mechanics to include art, astronomy, photography and many of the practical sciences. On his memorial cross he described himself with untypical economy as 'Engineer Astronomer Artist'. A more accurate description, perhaps, would be that of Victorian polymath. John Aldred has successfully captured the essential quality of the man and provided an excellent introduction to one of the most successful industrialists of the nineteenth century.

John A Cantrell
February 2008

Acknowledgements

My thanks are due to Dr John A Cantrell for his generosity in allowing me to use material from his published works in this more popular treatment of the Nasmyth story and for correcting my errors and omissions, to my wife Maureen and daughter Jill for proof reading and the general oversight of my efforts and to the Eccles and District History Society and the Eccles Community Committee for making it possible for this small book to appear in print.

chapter 1

The young James

You have probably heard of **Isambard Kingdom Brunel**, famous for designing and building railways, bridges and steamships, and you have probably come across the names of George and Robert Stephenson in connection with the Liverpool to Manchester railway, but have you heard of James Nasmyth?

Nasmyth was one of that great group of Victorian engineers who made technological leaps forward and in so doing revolutionised the engineering industry during the first half of the nineteenth century. In the process, he brought about the development of a tiny hamlet known as Patricroft on the outskirts of Eccles, about 5 miles (8 kms) west of Manchester, into a thriving industrial village. He was famous for building railway locomotives, for inventing and making a wide variety of machine tools and especially for his work in developing and manufacturing the steam hammer.

James was really left-handed but he was made to use his right hand so much when young that he became ambidexterous...

James was born in Edinburgh on the nineteenth of August 1808 of an old Scottish family. His father Alexander Nasmyth, born in 1758, began work as a coach painter. From this he moved on to portrait painting, became successful and painted many famous men including Robbie Burns. He next took up landscape painting with even greater success and eventually was labelled the "Father of Scottish Landscape Painting". He was also a talented draughtsman who had designed bridges and he had a workroom equipped with simple machine tools including a foot-lathe and an anvil. He also assisted an inventor called Patrick Miller with drawings connected with the use of steam power in ships. Following trials held on Dalswinton Loch in Scotland, Miller gave him £500.

It was a fairly affluent household visited by many famous men. Young James met the famous author Sir Walter Scott who gave him a coin for his collection and he even caught a glimpse of the eighty-year-old James Watt of steam engine fame.

James was the youngest surviving child of a large family, four boys and seven girls. He was the youngest boy separated by twenty years from the eldest child, Patrick, and he was especially close to his brother George who was two years older than himself. His full name was James Hall Nasmyth, called after his father's greatest friend Sir James Hall. James was really left-handed but he was made to use his right hand so much when young that he became ambidexterous; he used his left hand for drawing but manipulated machinery with his right. He was looked after by a nanny in his childhood and the

family employed other servants. When he was nine years old, he began to attend the Edinburgh High School where he proved an indifferent pupil. This followed an incident at a small school which he attended, run by a Mr Knight, in George St. Edinburgh, where his career almost came to an abrupt end when his teacher threw him against a wall with such force that he became unconscious. No action was taken by his father as the teacher apologised!! His brother George also attended the same school and was in fact in the same class. James preferred to spend his time turning spinning tops on his father's lathe as presents for his friends rather than attending school and he once made a small brass cannon which fired projectiles. The father of one of his close friends had a foundry and machine shop and here James learned to harden and temper steel. He made "steels"

By the time he was seventeen, he had made a small working steam engine from old files which, together with a flint, could be used to strike sparks to light a fire. The story goes that he used to use the gift of these to avoid punishment from Prefects at school.

He left school at the age of twelve in 1820, after which he was privately educated. In 1821 he enrolled at the Edinburgh School of Arts, which later became Herriot-Watt University where he attended evening classes in Mechanical Philosophy, Geometry, Mathematics and Chemistry. The model steam engines which he made so impressed Professor Leslie that he gave James free tickets to attend his lectures on Natural Philosophy. His father taught him drawing, a skill which he considered vital to any child's education and a tutor gave him lessons in mathematics. During the next few years James became increasingly interested in engineering and began to make his own tools in his father's workshop. By the time he was seventeen, he had made a small working steam engine to grind oil colours for his father's paints and he and his brother made a sectional model of Watt's steam engine for the Edinburgh School of Arts; for this they were paid ten pounds. He gave one third of his share of the money to his father for board and lodgings and the rest he spent on tickets to attend lectures at the University.

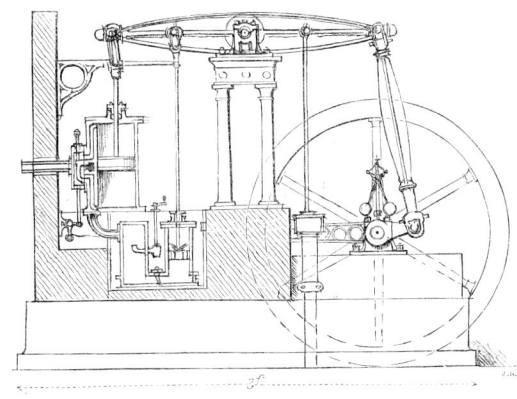

Sectional model of condensing steam-engine by James Nasmyth

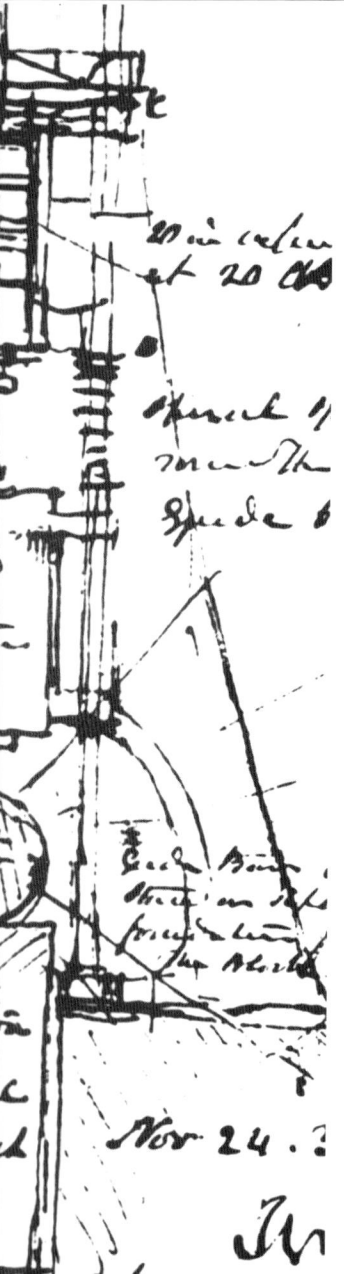

James was still living at home at this time and had problems finding areas in which to work. At one time he had a small brass foundry in his bedroom fireplace and used the bedroom carpet to deaden the sounds that might otherwise alert his mother to the fact that he was working late at night. If he needed larger tools he had the freedom of his friend's father's workshop which was only five minutes away. As his experience grew he attempted larger projects including making a steam-engine powerful enough to run a lathe and he was given orders for others.

When James was nineteen, the brothers made a small model steam carriage, a popular craze at the time, which was exhibited at the Scottish Society of Arts in Edinburgh. The Society were so impressed with the machine that they asked them to make a full-size version

Seven pounds profit for the Nasmyths!...

capable of carrying four to six people and allowed them £60 for materials. It took James and his brother about four months to build the machine but, when finished, it was capable of carrying eight passengers and crew on journeys of four or five miles (see drawing facing page 1). The castings for the machine were made at Anderson's foundry in Leith and one of their mechanics also helped in its construction. Eventually the Society gave the machine to James who broke it up for spare parts which he sold for £67, seven pounds profit for the Nasmyths!

In 1828, at the age of twenty, James contracted typhoid fever but, unlike Prince Albert who later in the century died from the disease, James made a full recovery.

It was perhaps during his illness that James had time to think about his future. He realised that he had a lot to learn and therefore decided to try to get an apprenticeship with his idol Henry Maudslay, a famous London engineer. Unfortunately when enquiries were made, it was discovered that Henry Maudslay did not take apprentices and in any case, at twenty years of age, James was too old for the traditional apprenticeship of seven years which usually started at about the age of fourteen.

chapter 2

James in London

Nothing daunted by these setbacks, James constructed a model steam-engine, assembled a portfolio of drawings and persuaded his father to ask a mutual friend for a letter of introduction to the Great Man. In 1829 James and his father sailed from Leith to London in a smack called the "Edinburgh Castle". After what must have been a very uncomfortable four days they reached the mouth of the Thames and sailed up from the Nore to London on a Saturday afternoon. The letter was delivered. The reply was discouraging but, not to let the young man down too heavily, Maudslay offered to take James and his father and possibly brother George on a tour of his works. James was delighted with everything that he saw. During the tour they came across a labourer, filthy and dressed in rags, raking out ashes from the fire box of a boiler and James is reputed to have said "if you would only permit me to do such a job as that in your service, I should

"I wish you to work, beside me, as my assistant workman. From what I have seen there is no need of an apprenticeship in your case"

consider myself most fortunate". Henry Maudslay was very impressed by this enthusiasm and offered to view the machine and drawings that the Nasmyths had brought to London. On the following day James and his father hired a handcart and took the offerings round to Henry Maudslay's factory where Henry refused to allow James to be present while he and his partner viewed the steam engine and drawings. James was on tenterhooks to know what Henry thought of his creations and was astounded and overjoyed when, after about twenty minutes, Henry Maudslay came out, took James into his private workshop and said "I wish you to work, beside me, as my assistant workman. From what I have seen there is no need of an apprenticeship in your case". Although there is no mention of the fact in James' autobiography there is evidence that his brother George also worked for Henry Maudslay at the same time as James. Both James and George were witnesses to Henry Maudslay's will dated December 1829.

Next came the hunt for somewhere to live. His father rejected one house because he saw "an ultra gay bonnet.....with flashy bright ribbons" lying on a bed and feared that female company might distract James from his studies. Eventually suitable accommodation was found and James began work on May 30th 1829, at the age of 20. It was decided that his pay should be ten shillings (50p) per week but the young man soon found that he could not afford to eat out very often on that wage. He therefore invented and constructed what we would nowadays call a slow cooker. It was made of sheet metal with a pan-like container on top and an oil lamp underneath. It

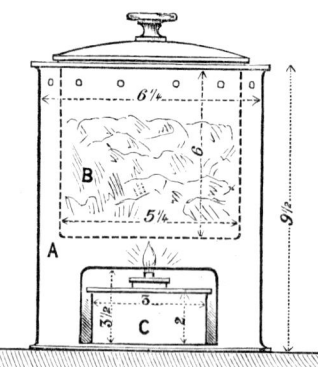

Cooking Apparatus
A-Cylindrical outer case
B-The meat pan, movable
C-Oil lamp

was made to James' design by a tinsmith in Lambeth and cost 6/- (30p). James claimed that "leg of beef", together with a helping of vegetables, all cooked together, cost him 4d (2p). If he prepared it before he went out to work in the morning it was beautifully cooked by the time he got back to his lodgings in the evening. He had three beef dinners a week and four meals of rice boiled with a few raisins and a pennyworth of milk. In 1830 his wages were increased to fifteen shillings (75p) per week, "then" said James "I had butter on my bread"! James worked very happily with Henry Maudslay who taught him almost all he knew about engineering.

Whilst living in Lambeth James met and became friendly with Michael Faraday, the famous chemist. During his spare time, James enjoyed walking round London and especially visiting Westminster Abbey to study its superb architecture. He also often visited the British Museum where he became especially interested in the Cuneiform inscriptions of the Assyrians and particularly how the indentations were produced in the clay tablets. He maintained this interest in later life and gave a lecture on the subject at the Royal Institution in 1839 and another to the British Association at Cheltenham in 1856. In 1825 whilst working for Maudslay, he became interested in applying steam power to the movement of barges along canals so that there was no damage to the banks. His method consisted of laying a chain along the bed of the canal which travelled over grooved rollers on a wheel driven by a small steam engine situated on the boat. The engine would then "walk" its way along the chain taking it up at the bow and dropping it again at the stern for the next barge to use. The method did not prove very practical at the time although a chainferry is now to be found on Lake Windermere in Cumbria.

In 1830 Maudslay went to Berlin to discuss designs for machines for the German Royal Mint, so James took the opportunity to visit the Liverpool to Manchester Railway where he made a drawing of what he thought was the famous "Rocket". In fact the engine that he drew was the "Northumbrian" which was very similar. He left London by stagecoach on Saturday 9th September 1830 and endured a miserably wet journey as far as Coventry where the sun appeared. He arrived in Liverpool on the Sunday night and took lodgings at a commercial hotel in Dale Street. During his stay in Liverpool he also visited the docks and a number of engineering works around the city. On Saturday 17th September 1830 he began to walk from Liverpool to Manchester and when he reached Patricroft, he sat down on the canal bridge to view the scene. He was

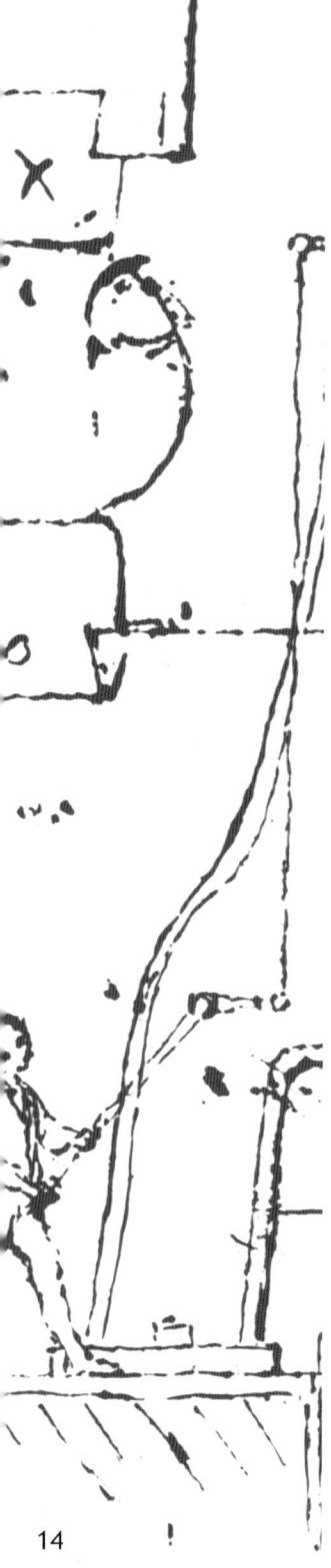

impressed by the rural aspect of the country and the ancient cottages of the neighbourhood. He noticed a piece of land which had the Bridgewater Canal on one side, the Liverpool-Manchester Railway on another and a good road on the third, a situation that he thought might be ideal for an engineering works. As in later life he contributed to the local Temperance Organisation in Patricroft, it is unlikely that he visited the Patricroft Tavern which had opened alongside the railway route at Patricroft in 1828. This is the earliest known example of a public house being deliberately sited to get trade from railway passengers. When Queen Victoria alighted from the train here in 1851 on her visit to Worsley, the Patricroft Tavern was renamed "The Queen's Head" but it continued to be known by the locals as the "Top House". The hotel is still in business although it is now called the "Queen's Arms."

He continued to Manchester where he stayed at the King's Arms on Deansgate and attended a service at the Cathedral on the following day. On the Monday he met Mr Edward Tootal, a wealthy mill owner of York Street, who showed him round some cotton mills. James was so impressed by the Manchester mill owners and merchants whom he met that he had his first thoughts that, at some time in the future, he might do well in the Manchester area.

He then made his way back to London visiting the "Black Country" of the Midlands on his way. He was deeply impressed by the noise and the vast scale of industry in the region which he probably regarded as signs of great prosperity, although he regretted the destruction of what had once been pleasant countryside. He was particularly impressed by the Soho works founded by Matthew Boulton in Birmingham. He was amazed at the size and complexity of the workshops and the amount of work being carried out. Nasmyth then retraced his steps to the south and said in his autobiography that he set out on his visit to the North with eight sovereigns in his pocket and arrived back as far as Windsor with one still intact. Rather than break into it he walked from there back to his lodgings in London, "without stopping for refreshment".

On February 14th 1831, Henry Maudslay died. James continued to work for Henry's partner Mr Field but, by 1831 when James was twenty-three years old, he began to feel that he was ready to start up in business for himself. To do this he would need to be equipped with the necessary machinery, so he and his brother returned to Edinburgh and set up an engineering business in 1833 at Old Broughton.

chapter 3

After Henry Maudslay

Back in Edinburgh, the Nasmyth brothers began work. They had with them castings of some of the best machines in Henry Maudslay's workshop with the blessing of Mr Field who was then the manager, to give them a start in the construction of the lathes and other equipment that they would need. They employed a mechanic called Archie Torrie who had worked as a mechanic for an iron company and had also been a millwright and therefore had the advantage of being a skilled woodworker as well as being competent in metal work. The brothers also took on an apprentice whose premium of fifty pounds a year paid Archie's wages. Once they felt equipped to start in business for themselves, the question was where? James visited Liverpool and took out an option to take over a foundry

---

They had with them castings of some of the best machines in Henry Maudslay's workshop

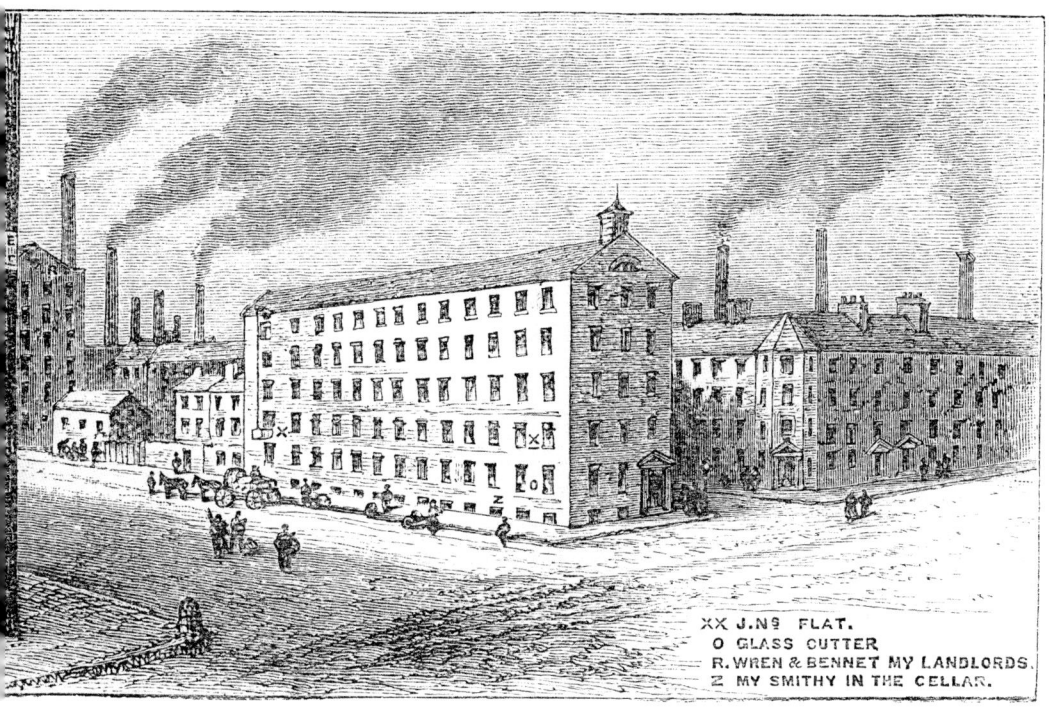

James' 1st workshop - a Dale St. Flat

but he eventually decided that Liverpool was not for him. With happy memories of the way he had been treated by the merchants of Manchester he decided that that was the place to be. He met a number of Manchester's leading industrialists including John Kennedy, William Fairbairn, the Grant brothers and Benjamin Hick of Bolton. Mr Tootal and others found them a "flat", actually a floor of a disused cotton mill in Dale Street, Piccadilly, where they could start in business. James was invited to dine with Mr Tootal and it was here that he met Daniel and William Grant. The Grants were the sons of a

Scottish herdsman who as young men, often barefoot, had driven cattle from Scotland to Cheshire. Eventually they had found work in Ramsbottom, invested their savings in cotton mills and finally became so wealthy that they were able to build a church for the people of Ramsbottom. The Grant brothers were said to have provided the model for the "Brothers Cheeryble" in Charles Dickens' "Nicholas Nickleby". Daniel and William were impressed with James' enthusiasm. They asked him how much capital he had and when James replied that he had sixty-three pounds, half of which belonged to his brother, they offered to make sure he would never be without funds on pay-day.

James sent for Archie Torrie and his equipment from Edinburgh and they started work. This was a boom time in engineering. Railway schemes were springing up all over the country and as the demand for labour exceeded the supply, the market for self-acting machines grew rapidly. Also, as James Nasmyth said, " machines did not get drunk either"! Their workshop produced drilling machines, planing machines, lathes and other machine tools.

Problems arose when they received an order for a large steam engine from an Irish firm. It was so large that it had to be made on its side and unfortunately the end of the engine beam crashed through the floor of the "flat" and debris of all kinds showered down into the glass merchant's premises on the floor below. It was obviously time to move.

chapter 4

James Nasmyth at Patricroft

Once again James thought of the site he had seen at Patricroft and wondered whether it was still vacant. He went to have another look, discovered that it was and that the owner was Squire Trafford. The brothers soon negotiated a 999 year lease at 1¾d (1p) a square yard on six acres (2.5 hectares) of land bounded by the Bridgewater Canal, the Liverpool-Manchester Railway and Green Lane. The site was ideal. Coal could be brought from Worsley by canal, there was brickclay on the site, there was solid sandstone underneath for sound foundations for buildings and the finished products could be carried away by rail, canal or road. Very soon a series of cheap wooden workshops covering about six acres were erected from pre-fabricated sections manufactured in Liverpool and by 1836 the Bridgewater Foundry was in business. James was just 28 years old and his brother was 30. In 1836 they leased a further 5,030 square yards (0.5 hectares)

It was surrounded by orchards and gardens which James said were "pleasant to pass after a hard day's work".

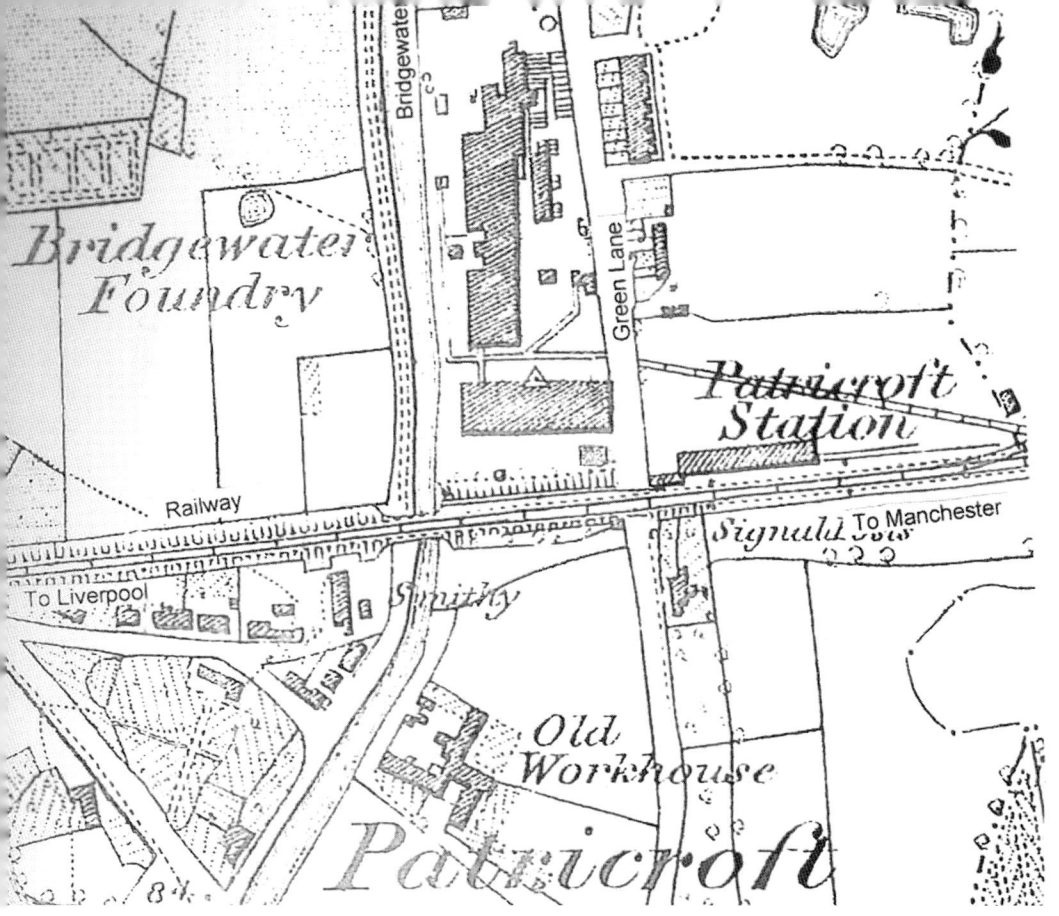

Bridgewater Foundry c1845- scale 1:3,000

from George Cornwall Legh. James' brother George was a very successful sales manager who was involved in the business until 1843 when he withdrew and set up in business for himself in London as a consulting engineer. James and George soon settled in at Patricroft; they were delighted by the greenness of the surrounding area of countryside and rented what James referred to as a "cottage" at Barton only six minutes away from the works, at a rent of £15 a year. It was surrounded by orchards and gardens which James said were "pleasant to pass after a hard day's work". One of their sisters came down from Edinburgh to look after them.

It is almost certain that what James called a "cottage" was in fact a sizeable house known as Green Lane House and which is now known as A.V. Roe House.

The canal wharf that James hoped to use for the import and export of his products belonged to the Bridgewater Trustees, whose agent James Southern, demanded a high rent for its use. Fortunately for James, Southern had to retire from his post due to his being involved in a dispute in the Chancery Court and James Loch was appointed to replace him, on behalf of Lord Francis Egerton of Worsley. Lord Francis came to visit the works, was delighted by the prospects of extra trade for the canal and offered to let James use the wharf free of charge; in fact James ended up paying a nominal rent of five shillings a year.

Lord Francis Egerton became the Earl of Ellesmere and used to bring visitors to the New Hall along the canal in his barge, to visit the foundry where he particularly enjoyed seeing fifteen or twenty tons of molten metal poured into moulds from a massive ladle. This was always a spectacular event accompanied by showers of red-hot sparks.

Self portrait aged 25 years, Sept 20 1837 Patrickcroft (sic)

There seem to have been problems with early orders and apparently the first three orders were cancelled, perhaps because of the time it took for the firm to become established. Once things settled down however, orders began in earnest and included one in 1837 for "a machine for squaring nut and bolt heads" for Caird & Co. engineers of Greenock in Scotland.

Expansion needed more workers and above all capital to pay wages and provide new buildings. The first large investors were Birley and Co., cotton manufacturers, who invested something like £40,000 in the enterprise by 1838, hoping for inventions that would provide new machines for the cotton trade. It

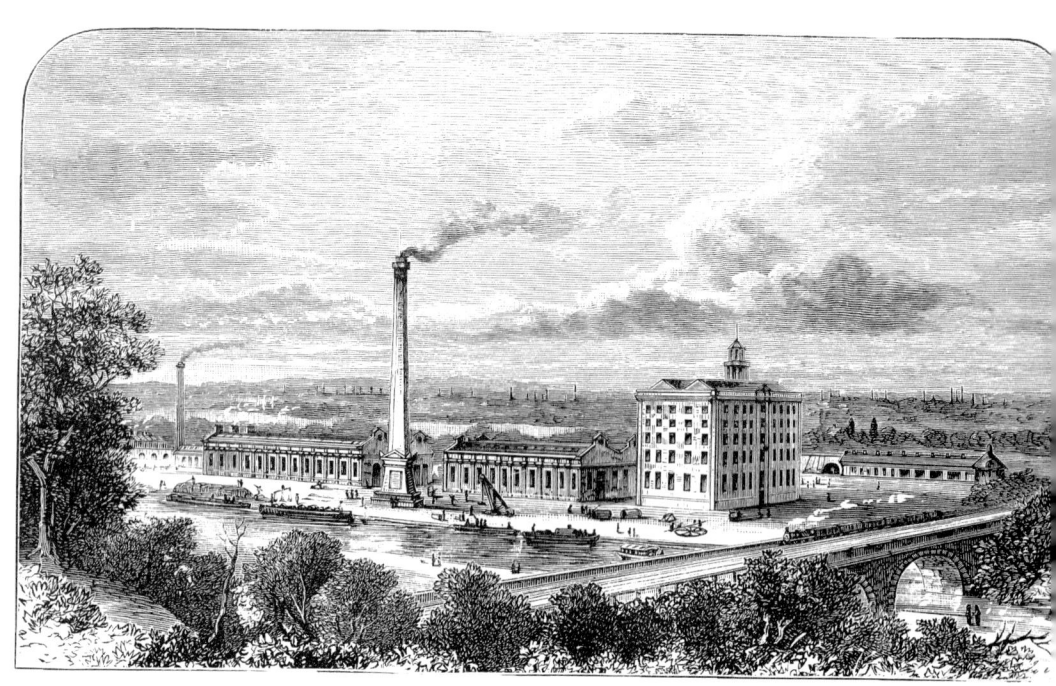

Bridgewater Foundry, Patricroft, from a painting by Alexander Nasmyth

is possible that when these seemed not to be forthcoming they withdrew their support. About the same time a man called Holbrook Gaskell joined the company, invested some capital, and took over the counting-house. This move was crucial to the sound development of the business because it was Gaskell who kept thorough records of orders and sales and made sure that the supplies they received were of the right quality and at the right price. He also made sure that all foreign orders were guaranteed by British banks and that credit was strictly controlled. Eventually the firm became

Nasmyth Gaskell and Co. as other investors were found. This partnership with Holbrook Gaskell meant that Nasmyth was free from the commercial affairs of the company and could devote all his time to the engineering side of the business. Gaskell remained with the firm until 1850 when he was hit on the head by a beam in an accident at the works. He was forced to retire but eventually recovered sufficiently to run an Alkali business in the Runcorn/Widnes area. In 1841 a further 46,463 sq. yards (about 10 acres or 4 hectares) of land on the east side of Green Lane was leased from Thomas Joseph Trafford to be used for workers' cottages and brick buildings began to spread over the site. On the west side of Green Lane the building nearest to Patricroft was of a five-storey construction which was most unusual for an engineering works. It is said that this pattern was forced upon James by some investors who, if James' business failed, hoped to recoup their capital by converting the building into a cotton mill. It was known by the workers as the "Weaving Shed" even though no weaving was ever done there.

With true Scottish thrift no part of the newly acquired land was allowed to remain idle. The accounts include an entry in 1837 for manuring the 3rd field at a cost of 2/6d (12½p) and in the same year there is an entry for carrying "hay seed from Barton Locks" to Patricroft. Farming of surplus land continued for a number of years and even in 1846 on July 7th, there is an entry "for Derbyshire 300 sprinklers (pegs?) To thatch haystack." There is also a record of a payment of 11/- (55p) paid to "Henry Hindley for seven gallons of ale for the hay

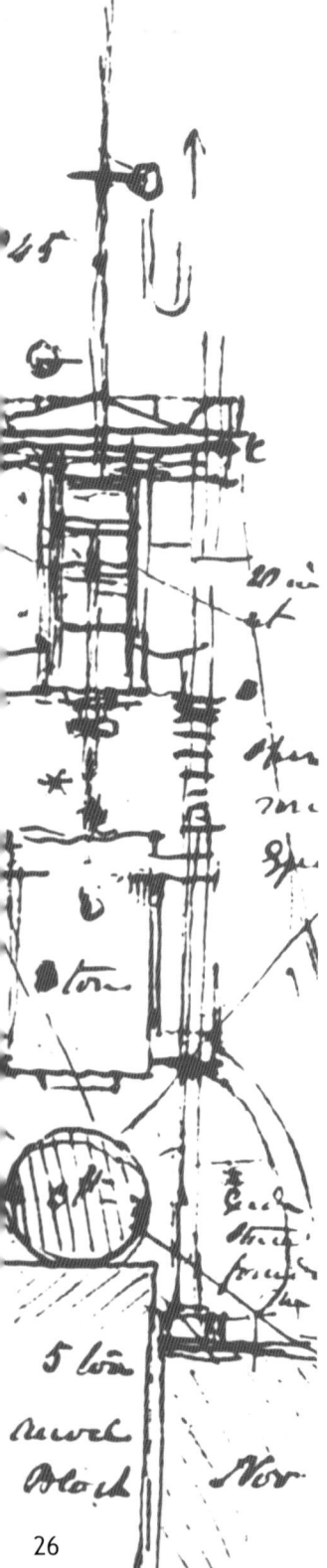

makers". Obviously thirsty work! To even matters out, James paid out £4 0s 0d to renew his subscription to the Temperance Institute on an annual basis.

The new works made full use of supplies of raw materials that were available locally. A payment was made to "the brickmaker for moulding bricks" on site and from clay dug within the boundaries of the enterprise. Red moulding sand which was needed in large quantities, seems to have been obtained from a quarry near Eccles Old Road not far from where Salford Royal (Hope) Hospital now stands. There is a mention in the accounts for 1844 of an allowance paid to Lancaster's carter for bringing a load of red sand when the ground was covered with snow; he "had a rough job" states the record. He was allowed the princely sum of 2½d (1p) for his trouble! As early as 1837 coal was being brought by water from Worsley. There is a mention in the accounts of 6d (2½p) as an allowance for "the Coal Boat man" probably after a particularly heavy or dirty cargo. There is also a later mention of coal being brought from Poynton in Cheshire. Large quantities of horse manure were used in the foundry. In 1838 there is a record of "Horse Dung (via old woman) 6d" (2½p) and again in the same year, "5 barrows per man 2/6d" (12½p), a frequently repeated entry. In the same year quantities of old shoes were bought on a number of occasions. One entry was for "37 lbs (about 17 kilos) at ½d per pound, 3/1d" (15p). These were used in the case-hardening of metals. There is an interesting entry, once again for 1838 when 1¾ cwts (about 90 kilos) of "Old wrought iron" was bought from the Workhouse. Whether this was the result of demolition or whether this was the result of scavenging by the inmates is unknown. Supplies of Pig Iron had to be imported from further afield and on January 15th 1854, "H.S. to Runcorn to ascertain when Pig Iron could be got here by canal" is another interesting entry in the works accounts. Security at this time seems to have been in the hands of the traditional "man and his dog". In 1838 a "cape for the Watchman" was priced at 10/- (50p) and "Meat and bread for the dog" cost 3/1d (16p). Whether or not they were successful in deterring intruders is not recorded.

By 1838 the Nasmyth works were capable of building railway locomotives and the company quickly established a reputation for craftsmanship and reliability. In 1838/39 the first locomotive was built which was called "Bridgewater". It was a 2-2-2 type which means that there were two wheels in front of two driving wheels followed by two non-driving wheels, with a four-wheeled tender. The driving wheels were five feet in diameter. It was tried out on the Liverpool-Manchester railway in March 1839 where it proved capable of

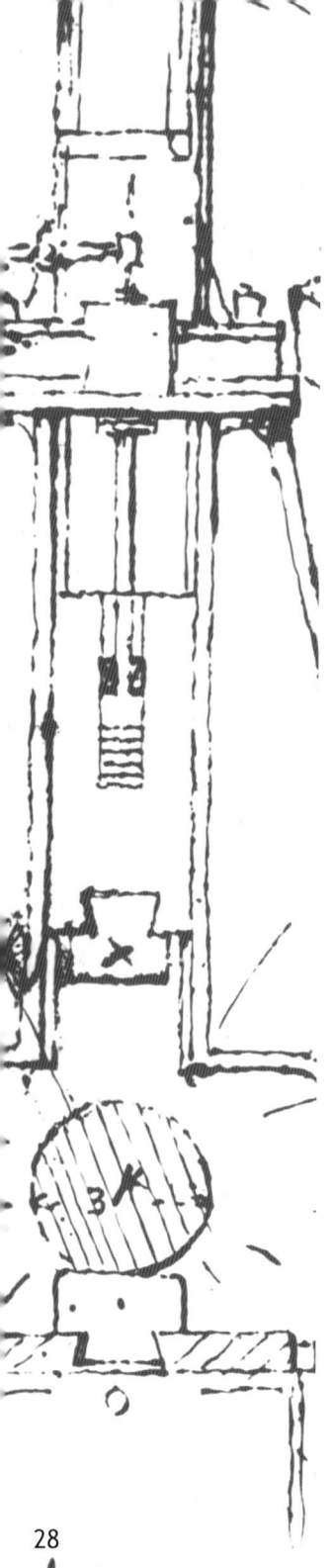

carrying 100 tons at more than 20 miles per hour. A letter from James Nasmyth to the secretary of the railway company describes the engine as being "built on Mr Stephenson's principle ie with 6 wheels and outside framing and is of substantial yet elegant construction". Despite the offer of a week's free loan, the Liverpool to Manchester Railway Co. did not buy the machine and it was not sold until 1841 when it was bought for use on the Manchester to Birmingham railway. Three more engines were built for the London and Southampton Railway in 1838 called "Hawk", "Falcon" and "Raven". These were designs by Edward Bury and their tenders were made at the Clarence Foundry in Liverpool. In 1839 nine locomotives were built and in 1840 thirteen. In 1841 eight and in 1842 sixteen locomotives were constructed, some of which were supplied to George and Robert Stephenson. The export of locomotives to a variety of countries including India, Russia, Australia, New Zealand, Spain and South America was always important. Between 1837 and 1939 when the last engine was built, 1,260 engines were exported out of a total of 1,632 constructed.

James Nasmyth was often at loggerheads with organised labour. He believed that negotiations about wages and conditions of work should be carried out between him and his workforce without the intervention of an organisation such as a Trade Union. Speaking before a Commission on Trade Unions in 1868 he said "The intrusion of any third party is… derogatory to the interests of society at large and to trade in particular". He also did not agree with the apprentice system. He said that apprenticeship agreements made boys lazy so he paid what an individual was worth on a day-to-day basis.

As the company grew, men were recruited from Liverpool, Manchester and the surrounding districts to swell the workforce and many of these men were keen Trade Unionists. They waited until a particularly large order had been received at the works and then a deputation from the Engineering Mechanics Trade Union went to James and declared that many of Nasmyth's workers were not "legally entitled to the trade", because they had not served a proper apprenticeship. The Union demanded that these men be sacked and union members appointed in their place; if this was not done strike action would be taken. James refused their request and over half his workers walked out on strike. No other labour was available locally and the order was waiting to be filled but James soon decided on a solution to the problem. He advertised for workers in Edinburgh and selected over sixty

men keen to move to Patricroft. They arrived at Liverpool closely followed by their families, walked to Patricroft and confronted the pickets who were said to have been dumbfounded. They brushed the pickets aside and entered the works. The story goes that the newcomers evicted the strikers from their cottages and that their families moved in to take their place. There is some doubt about this as Nasmyth's autobiography merely states that the incomers found lodgings nearby and it is not certain that worker's cottages had been built by this date. James later said that there were several Worsley men whom he had employed first as labourers and whom, when their skills had increased, he had promoted to mechanics without the need of a formal apprenticeship. He cited James Brindley and James Watt neither of whom had served apprenticeships, in defence of his actions. As James himself said, his watchword was "Free Trade in Ability". There was of course great illfeeling in the neighbourhood among union members and the Bridgewater employees were "blacked" from obtaining other jobs in the area for a long time afterwards.

'Fireside' after a drawing by James Nasmyth showing telescope

In 1838 James went to Sheffield on business and the coach back to Manchester was delayed by deep snow. Rather than waste his time, he went to Barnsley to visit an iron works managed by a Mr Hartop who was one of Nasmyth's customers. During his two-day stay in Barnsley he met Mr Hartop's daughter Anne and was so taken with her that at the end of his stay he asked Anne's father's permission to propose marriage. This was allowed and it was agreed that "if business continues to progress favourably, our union should take place in about two years". It did and they were married on June

16th 1840 and, after a honeymoon in the Lake District, they went to live in Winton House, also known as Ellesmere House. This was a large building in its own grounds with a main entrance from Worsley Road. It was about 300 yards (275 m) from the works as the crow flies. In 1842 they moved into a large house in Patricroft called "Fireside", situated between what is now the north end of Legh Street and the canal. James' father had died in 1840 so after his marriage James' mother and unmarried sisters moved into Green Lane House (A.V. Roe House) from Edinburgh to care for James' brother George. When George left for London in 1843 Mrs Nasmyth and her daughters moved to Richmond Terrace, Pendleton, near to the house of her married daughter Anne, where she remained until her death in 1847.

The railway-engine business grew rapidly. The company tendered successfully for twenty engines on the seven-foot gauge for the Great Western Railway and got a premium of £100 on each for reliable running. This was a period of railway mania in Britain; six hundred and seventy-one Railway Acts were passed by Parliament between 1845 and 1848. They built engines which were sometimes to Nasmyth designs but more often they were made to designs supplied with the order. In all, 109 locomotives were built in the years between 1838 and 1853.

The production of steam engines and other tools also continued to increase. The company began to manufacture machines for compressing cotton into bales enabling as many as eighty-five bales to be processed in one hour. There was soon a great demand for these from India and Egypt which were expanding the production of cotton for export at that time. James was also the inventor of a safety ladle for pouring molten metal which required fewer men and gave much greater control than the previous system had done. Nasmyth's was one of the first firms to use in-line or what might now be called flow-line working. Wooden patterns for castings were made at one end of the building and castings were then made next door in the foundry. After that came the machine shop and finally the finished machine moved into the packing department for despatch by rail, canal or later by road. In 1839 a sales catalogue was issued containing no fewer than fifty tools which were available to buy.

chapter 5

James Nasmyth and the Steam Hammer

In 1839 Isambard Kingdom Brunel was appointed engineer-in-charge of the project to build the famous steamship the "Great Britain" at Bristol. It was to be a paddle steamer but nothing as large as the wrought-iron paddle shaft needed to power the ship had ever been forged. Nasmyth was consulted by Mr Humphries a consultant engineer on the project and as James said later, "within half an hour of his leaving I had made a steam-powered hammer sketch in my design book" which he thought capable of doing the job. He submitted his design to the steamship company in Bristol and it was approved. Sadly, before either the steam hammer or the shaft could be made, the method of propulsion for the ship was changed to propeller-drive so neither was required.

Did James Nasmyth invent the steam hammer? A headline in the Eccles and Patricroft Journal of 9th September

"within half an hour of his leaving I had made a steam-powered hammer sketch in my design book"

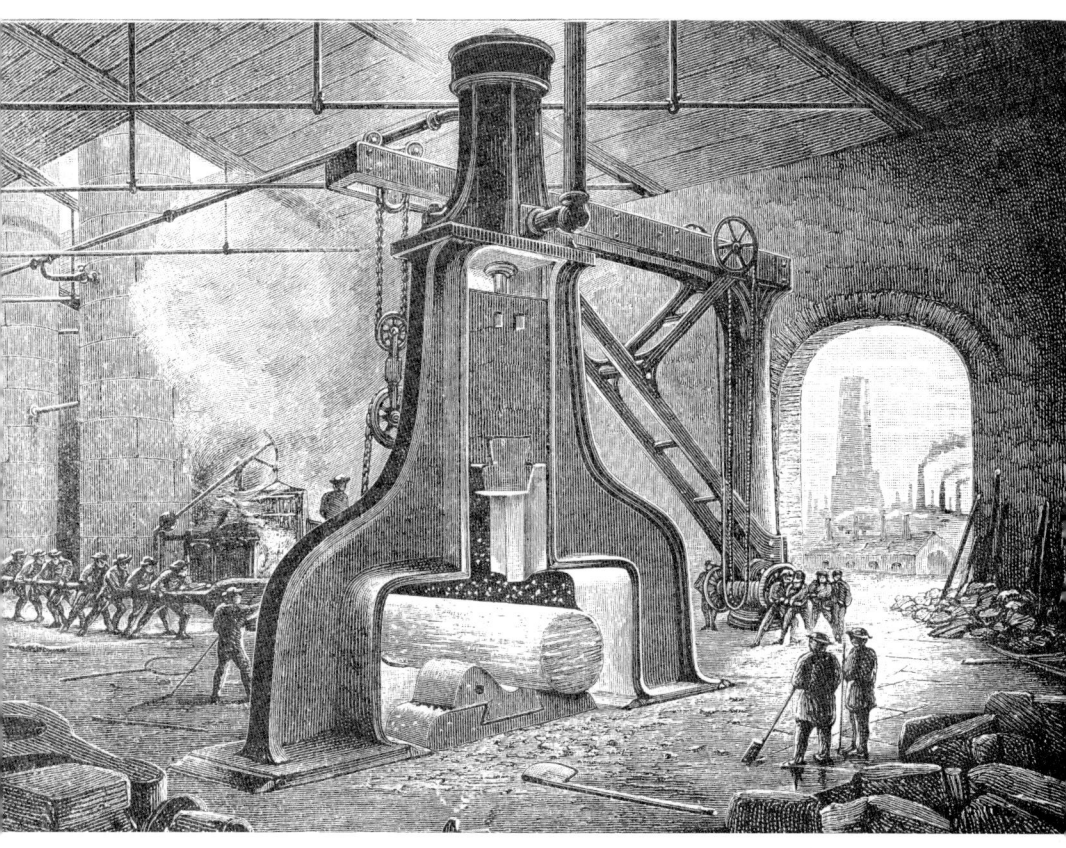
Steam Hammer in full work - from a painting by James Nasmyth

1982 claimed "Every true Eccles person knows that James Nasmyth invented the steam hammer". Queen Victoria also thought he did and he is credited with the invention in most British encyclopaedias; the truth of the matter is not quite so clear cut. A French engineer called Bourdon, who worked for Schneider Bros. and Co at Le Creusot in central France, visited the Patricroft works at a time when James was absent. He was shown round by Holbrook Gaskell and saw Nasmyth's design book which included his sketch of plans for a steam hammer. Some time later, Nasmyth returned

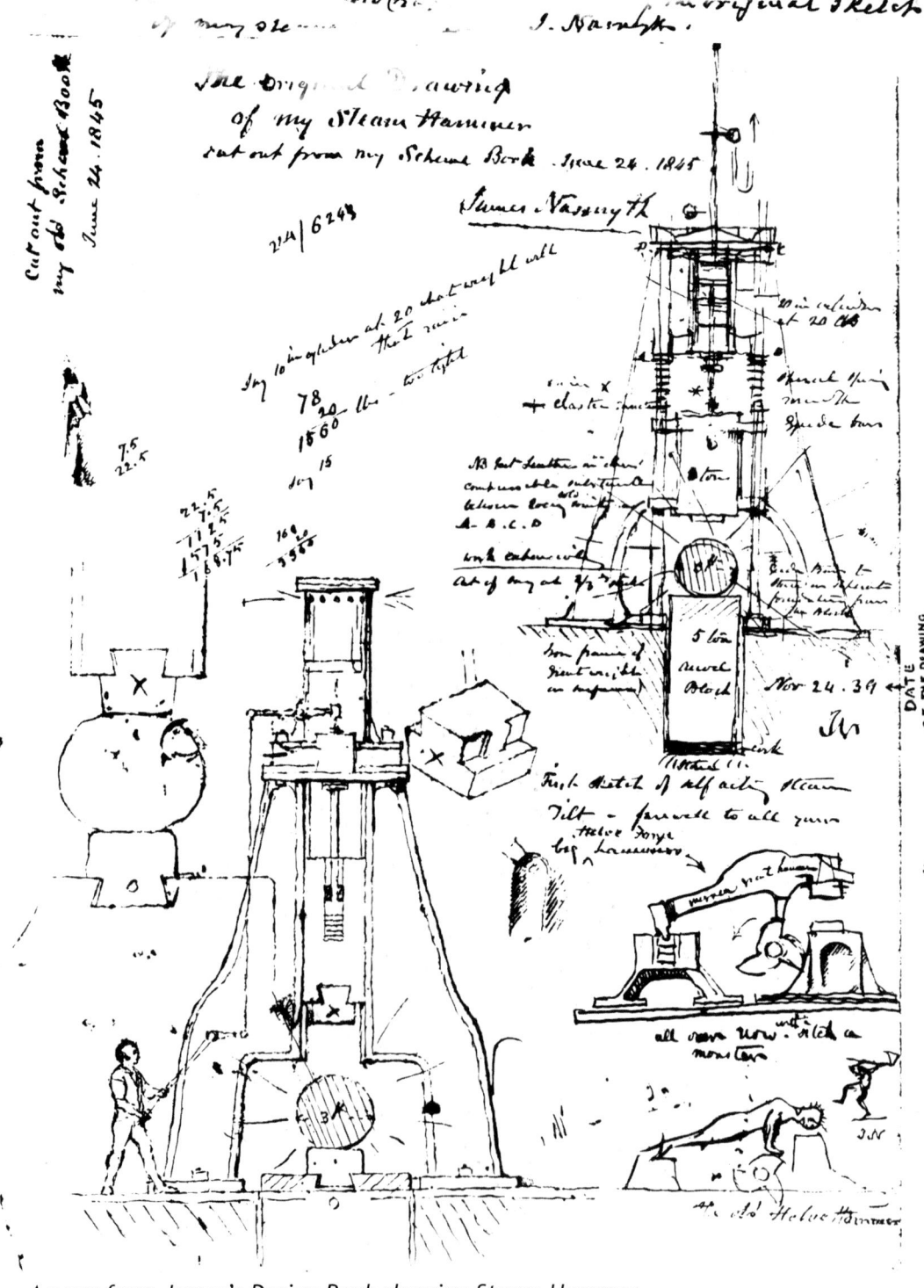

A page from James's Design Book showing Steam Hammer.

Bourdon's visit and was amazed when he saw in the works a steam hammer looking very like the one in his sketch book, which he had never built. The French firm had patented its hammer in 1842. Recriminations followed and James hurried home to patent almost every aspect of his steam-hammer project. He patented an invention which would make "certain improvements in machinery or apparatus for forging, stamping and cutting iron and other substances" in June 1843.

Modern research has clarified the situation to a degree. It seems fair to say that the idea of a steam hammer was probably British and existed before Nasmyth's time, but as no large forgings had ever been required, no machine had been constructed. James Watt and an engineer named Deverell had considered the problem of using steam to raise a hammer early in the nineteenth century but no practical machines were ever constructed. It is also likely that Bourdon had some designs of his own before he visited Nasmyth, but he did see James' design book. Experts maintain however that the sketch Bourdon saw was not sufficiently detailed to enable him to build a steam hammer from that alone. It might well also be true that it was the sight of James' drawings that spurred Bourdon on to build a machine; it is also true that Nasmyth did not actually build a steam hammer until he had seen the one that Bourdon had constructed.

A fair conclusion, as with many inventions, is to say that credit for the final development of the steam hammer during the 1830/1840 period should probably be shared between

Britain and France. In 1871 the French firm challenged Nasmyth's right to claim that he had invented the steam hammer before a select committee of the House of Commons on Patent Law; they claimed that Nasmyth had copied the French design but no firm conclusion was reached.

Once steam hammers went into production, they became very popular and hundreds were made of all sizes. The basic principle on which they worked was that steam was used to lift the hammer which then fell by gravity; later, steam was used to push the hammer down as well. Many improvements were made, not least a self-acting mechanism developed by James' Works Manager Robert Wilson which greatly improved the machine's efficiency. Nasmyth never gave Robert Wilson the credit he deserved for this

a gift of £1 was made to Joy's foreman and another £1 was shared among "Joy's men"

important development. James used to take great pride in demonstrating the delicacy with which a hammer could be controlled by cracking the shell of an egg in a wineglass, using a two-ton machine, without breaking the glass.

At one time to manufacture drive shafts of 15 or 20 cwts was thought an outstanding achievement but the new steam hammers made it possible to produce shafts of 20 or 30 cwts with relative ease. Between 1843 and 1856 five hundred hammers were sold, together worth over £200,000. The Board of Ordnance bought 61 and many were sold abroad in France, Italy and Spain. There is little doubt that the profits from the sale of steam hammers were the foundation of Nasmyth's fortune. One of the problems with the construction of the steam hammer was the difficulty of casting the "hammer sides". These had to be flawless if they were to withstand the shock of the hammer falling on the anvil. There is a record in the accounts for April 29th 1854 showing "gift to moulders by Mr Nasmyth for six good hammer sides - 15/-"(75p), obviously an event worth celebrating. The installation of a hammer was not without expense. Jas Stewart was paid 35 days' allowance to cover the cost of his board, which cost 1/4d (7p) per day, when erecting "Joy's hammer" in 1843, and when Nasmyth went to Manchester "to start Joy's hammer", a gift of £1 was made to Joy's foreman and another £1 was shared among "Joy's men". Was this to encourage future orders? On February 1st 1844 there is a record of "a present to Rushton's forgeman on starting the hammer," so obviously these "sweeteners" were common practice.

chapter 6

Business expands

A visit to Patricroft by the Grand Duke Constantine of Russia resulted in orders for rope-making equipment but a return visit to Russia by Nasmyth had to be abandoned because of the Crimean War. Workers at Patricroft went on strike in 1842 as part of a nation-wide General Strike called in support of the Chartist movement which was endeavouring to obtain voting rights for all males. One of the fifty-eight Chartists accused of "seditious conspiracy" was a mechanic who worked at the Bridgewater foundry.

In 1848, Nasmyth was asked to review the machinery used at the Government Arsenal at Woolwich. He reported that the machinery then in use was out of date and of course got the contract to supply replacements. He was also involved in a number of relatively local engineering projects. On December 27th 1847 Nasmyth went to the Manchester Infirmary to attend a meeting on ventilation and on October 30th 1848, James claimed the sum of 1/- (5p) for the fare to Victoria Station in Manchester when he went "to take a plan of the roof". In the next year, on February 27th, he travelled to Birkenhead and "to Seacombe to examine the landing stage with Mr Brown etc". On his return he submitted a claim for one day's expenses at 19/9d (97p).

As early as 1850, Nasmyth's were producing coal gas for fuel at the works. In May 1850 there is an entry in the accounts which states, "W.Worth 2 yards canvas to mend top of the Gasometer" and in December of the same year a payment was made to "Satterfield - time for gasmaking 2/2d" (11p), presumably as being extra to his normal work.

The general business of the company continued to expand. James travelled abroad visiting dockyards in France at Marseille and Toulon. He went to Italy where he saw Vesuvius and Pompeii; wherever he went, orders followed. In 1842 he travelled with Holbrook Gaskell to Nuremburg in Germany in connection with railway orders and then visited firms in Denmark, Sweden and St Petersburg in Russia.

Nasmyth realised that the steam hammer principle could be applied to other situations, especially pile driving. The standard pile used in dock construction at that time was of wood 70 feet (21.3ms) long and 18 inches (45 cms) square. Using traditional methods it took twelve hours to drive one pile into place but in 1845, Nasmyth built a pile driver which

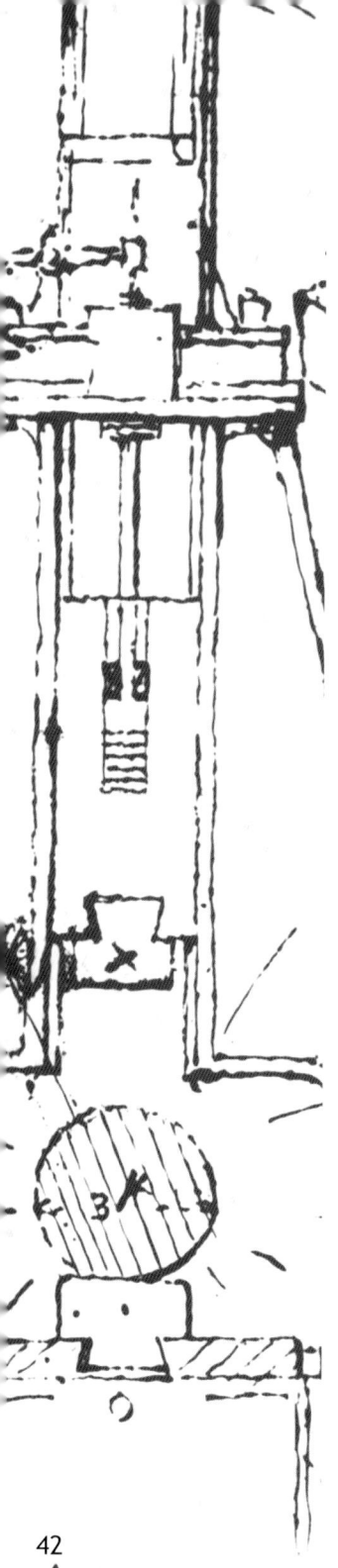

drove one of these piles into place in four and a half *minutes* with a four-ton block and at the rate of eighty strokes a minute. He proved the efficiency of his equipment in a competition with a conventional pile driver and won hands down. Orders came from Egypt where they were used in the construction of a Nile Dam at Cairo, from Newcastle-on-Tyne where they helped to build the high-level bridge and many other projects world-wide.

Engineering in the nineteenth century was a dangerous business and accidents were common. At 12.55 p.m. on June 14th 1845 disaster struck part of the works. The water level in the boiler of a steam engine had been allowed to get too low and the resultant high pressure caused the boiler to burst. The end of the boiler lifted, swung round demolishing two chimneys and then it went broadside pushing a four-ton steam hammer into the canal. Thousands of bricks fell, two men were killed, many were buried or scalded and a five year old child was killed by a flying slate outside the works. About £2,000 worth of damage was caused.

The firm's accounts record the treatment of many accidents, which varied from a minor burn to death, in a number of ways. In 1837 there is a record of brandy being provided for " J.Leach's accident 1/3d" (6p). In 1838 sticking plaster for bruises was paid for and in 1840 brandy was again provided, this time for a broken leg and also for a "man with a bruised hand". A more serious accident on December 30th 1844 resulted in a payment of 10d (4p) for turnpike tolls for what must have been an agonising journey "to the Infirmary with Wilkinson Forgeman's thigh broken at the hammer". He was conveyed in Thomas Moor's spring cart, obviously the nearest thing they had to a works ambulance, at a cost of 2/6d (12½p). On June 18th 1845, a donation of 10/- (50p) was made to Stephen Barr "to assist him to Scotland"; he was "hurt in the back when Rodger's boiler exploded on the 14th". This was a serious accident as, on June 23rd "Gift to widow of Davies, fitter, who died from wound to the thigh received when Roger's boiler exploded - 5/3½d making with his wages 20/- (£1)", was recorded. Hardly a princely sum!! Evidence of other boiler disasters can be found in the accounts. On October 30th 1847, there is a record of "W.N's expenses attending investigation of late boiler explosion at New Hey Mills, Rochdale and giving evidence in a Coroner Inquest". This was not a unique occurrence. On another occasion in 1849 leeches were provided at a cost of 2/3d (11p) for "Pollit who was hurt by the falling of the remainder of the Old Boiler House shed roof". Whether they did him any good or not is not recorded.

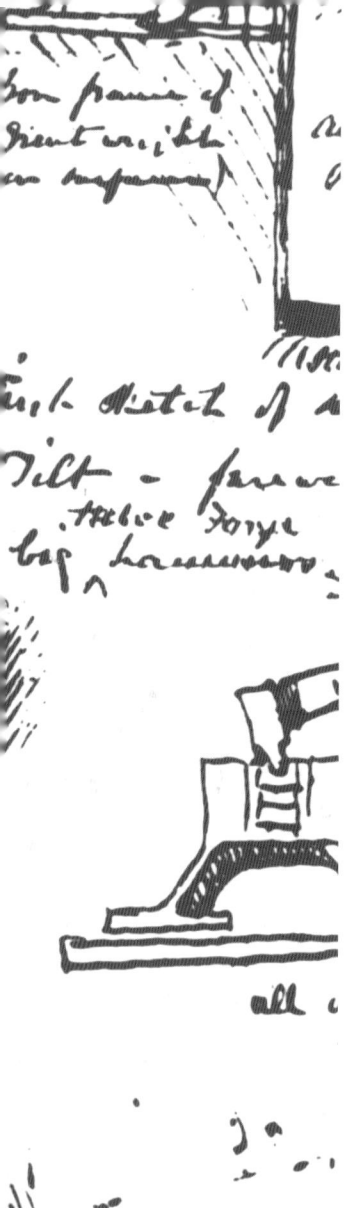

Although James was a fair employer he followed the wages and practices of the time. A labourer was paid three shillings (15p) per week but if he had the skill he could progress to become a mechanic earning thirty-five shillings (£1.75) a week. Work began at six in the morning and went on until eight in the evening - sometimes later - and they worked six days a week for fifty-two weeks a year. In his autobiography James made his view on wages very clear. He said "once labourers get more than a living wage - drunkenness and absenteeism resulted". No wonder he was not popular with

> "once labourers get more than a living wage - drunkenness and absenteeism resulted"

the Unions! Despite this strictness, the records show many small acts of kindness to workers. Gifts of ale to men doing unusually arduous jobs were common. "Clarke's Dinner Basin - broken in the yard" was replaced at a cost of 1½ d (2p) and a "foot bear" (foot muff) was provided for use in what was obviously a very cold office. In 1850 the sum of six shillings (30p) was paid as "expenses of summons by John Oswald and Thomas Brownsword for wages short paid viz. the amount received from each for rent on Jan. 26th which Mr Trafford, Magistrate at Worsley, decided ought not to have been stopped as the men were not told when they were engaged that they would be required to take and pay for a cottage". At a time when employment legislation was in its infancy, this was a major victory for the "working man". Mr Trafford was obviously a fair minded and conscientious magistrate.

Commemorative plaque recording engines built by Nasmyth - Gaskell and co. 1841-1842

chapter 7

Pastimes and hobbies

Despite the problems of a large work force and a prosperous company, or possibly as a distraction from these responsibilities, James had a number of hobbies. His father had taught him to draw and he also developed a passion for astronomy. He manufactured metal mirrors for telescopes including one which was ten inches (25 cms) in diameter for a reflecting telescope for his own use. He set it up in the garden at "Fireside" where his late night observations, while dressed in his night shirt, scared a passing boatman who claimed that he had seen a ghost. In 1842 he began to survey the moon and made drawings and maps of its surface which were shown at a meeting of the British Association in Edinburgh where they generated great interest.

His father had taught him to draw and he also developed a passion for astronomy.

A drawing by James Nasmyth titled "The Fairies"

In 1850 preparations were being made for the Great Exhibition of Trade and Industry which was to be held in London in 1851. James was appointed an Area Commissioner, one of a number of people throughout the country whose job was to see that all areas were fairly represented. From his own firm he submitted a 30cwt steam hammer, a compact steam engine that could propel a ship and maps of the moon. He eventually received medals for all three of his entries.

Prince Albert was particularly interested in the maps of the moon. When he visited Worsley New Hall with Queen Victoria in 1851 as part of a visit to Liverpool and Manchester, he asked the Earl of Ellesmere to invite James to show them his lunar studies. A charming letter exists from Lady Harriet Ellesmere to James Nasmyth which begins "My dear Sir, I have ascertained that the Queen and Prince Albert would have great pleasure in seeing your drawings and maps of the moon and hearing your explanation of them". It then went on to invite James to "give them the pleasure of his company after dinner on the day of arrival (October 9th) and will you bring with you your drawings?" Both he and Mrs Nasmyth were also invited to "pass the

"My dear Sir, I have ascertained that the Queen and Prince Albert would have great pleasure in seeing your drawings and maps of the moon and hearing your explanation of them"

evening here" on October 10th. In her diary Queen Victoria remarked "the evening was enlivened by Mr Nasmyth, the inventor of the steam hammer...he exhibited and explained his maps and drawings of the surface of the moon". She also described him as having a charming manner which combined "simplicity, modesty and enthusiasm of genius". James also managed to interest the Earl of Ellesmere in astronomy and gave him advice on the design and erection of a telescope for his own use. A letter from the Earl to James dated November 7th 1848 shows the Earl to be preparing a stone base for a large telescope to be erected at one of his country houses. There is also evidence that he installed a large telescope at Worsley New Hall. The same letter discusses a report of the apparent sighting of a "monster" by the sailing ship Daedalus. The Earl seriously suggests that what had been seen by the ship's crew must have been a Plesiosaurus and goes on to say, "If I am right, there is yet a possibility of seeing the monster on land for the plesiosaurus was at least as capable of climbing on a rock as the seal". Shades of the Loch Ness monster!

chapter 8

Retirement

In 1856, at the age of forty-eight, after a business career lasting only twenty-two years, James Nasmyth retired from the company. It is not known why; fatigue or trouble with the unions have been suggested as possible reasons or it might have been that by that time James had achieved his major ambitions and could retire a wealthy man. By now the Bridgewater Foundry was extremely well established. James claimed that, when he retired, he was leaving full order books and 630 regular customers. He left the firm in the sole control of his then partner Henry Garnet who took in his two sons and Robert Wilson. The Bridgewater Foundry section of the firm was then called "The Patricroft Iron Works" until 1867 when it was renamed "Nasmyth Wilson & Co".

a business career lasting only twenty-two years

James and his wife left "Fireside" at Patricroft and settled at Penshurst in Kent. Their new home was called "Hammerfield", a very suitable name for a house lived in by the Nasmyths. Here he had workshops, a studio, a library and extensive gardens. While the house was being prepared for their occupation, James and his wife rented a house, for six months, at Sydenham in Kent, near the Crystal Palace. They enjoyed attending daily orchestral concerts and referred to this period as a "happy episode".

In retirement he devoted himself to his hobbies. He lectured on the moon, visited Italy and France with his wife Anne and published a book entitled "The Moon, considered as a Planet, a World, and a Satellite " which was well thought of by the astronomers of the day. He also began to dabble in photography.

Little is known about him from then on but recent research has unearthed the fact that, at about the time of his retirement, he embarked on an affair with a lady called Virtue Squibb who, under the name of Emily Russel, was set up in a smart house in Pimlico, in London. The affair continued for over twenty years until her death in 1885 and the result of this relationship was an illegitimate daughter, Minnie, who lived until 1940. How he came to meet Virtue Squibb is not clear. James made over the sum of £1,000, in a bond which should have produced about £30 a year, to their daughter Minnie on the death of her mother, using the name James James rather than James Nasmyth. The few surviving letters from James to

Virtue to arrange meetings in London are mawkishly sentimental and completely at odds with the side of his character seen by the workaday world where he appeared dour and single-minded in business.

It seems likely that, despite the length of the relationship, James' wife Anne remained completely ignorant of this second household and had a happy, if childless, life with her husband.

The reason why so little mention is made of "Brother George" is that later in life he became the black sheep of the family. He was appointed the first curator of the Patent Museum in 1857 but in 1859 he was suspended "on suspicion of appropriating to his own use the public money entrusted to him" and he was dismissed later that year. He left the country shortly afterwards and was last heard of in America where he died in Louisville, Kentucky, in 1862.

James Nasmyth, according to his death certificate, died on May 7th 1890, aged eighty-one, at Bailey's Hotel in South Kensington in London. His will provided handsomely for his widow and after this bequest there was still about £250,000 left mostly invested in 3% consols which James said did not pay a high rate of interest but were very secure; most of this he left to charity. Another section of his will stipulated that he wished to be cremated and that his ashes should be interred in Edinburgh. Cremation was very unusual at that time as the first crematorium, at Woking, was only opened in 1879, but his wishes were carried out. The story goes that at that time human ashes in an urn were charged at full fare on the railway as if they were a corpse so James' remains travelled to Edinburgh in May 1890, by train, free of charge in an urn in a brown paper parcel! They were buried in a small cemetery two miles outside Edinburgh in the village of Dean.

The "Volcano" - a steam-sloop fitted by Nasmyths as a floating factory to service the Russian Baltic fleet

James was not only a national but also an international figure. A measure of his fame in Britain was given by the fact that on January 27th 1883 the satirical magazine "Punch" published a full-page cartoon in its "PUNCH'S FANCY PORTRAITS - No. 120." series showing James Nasmyth's head between the hammer and anvil of a simple steam hammer. The tall hat that he often wore was represented by the cylinder of the hammer and the god Vulcan stands by holding an assortment of hammers and pincers. Underneath the cartoon is the name "James Nasmyth" and below that is the caption "The Man Who Knows How To Knock Metal On The Head With The Right Hammer!" The page is finished off with a mock quotation from Shakespeare's "The Life and Death of King John" Act IV Scene ii saying "I saw Nasmyth ('a smith' in the original) stand with his hammer thus!" (Mr Punch's edition).

"The Man Who Knows How To Knock Metal On The Head With The Right Hammer!

PUNCH'S FANCY PORTRAITS.—No. 120.

JAMES NASMYTH.

THE MAN WHO KNOWS HOW TO KNOCK METAL ON THE HEAD WITH THE RIGHT HAMMER!

"I saw Nasmyth stand with his hammer thus!" King John. act iv, sc.2ii (Mr Punch's edition) Jan1883

J.Nasmyth as seen by "Punch"

chapter 9

Conclusion

So here ends the story of a remarkable man. Although he was determined in business and single-minded in dealing with competition he was often described as charming by a variety of people. Physically he was short and thick-set with a prominent nose which he understandably reduced in his self portrait, and thick curly hair. He was credited not only with the development of the steam hammer but with over forty other inventions. These ranged from a cotton-baling machine for India and a wide variety of machines for planing and shaping metal, to a floating gun. The firm also manufactured and supplied lathes and other equipment for the Volcano, a ship which enabled the Russian navy to service its Baltic Sea fleet while at sea.

Physically he was short and thick-set with a prominent nose

Early twentieth-century advertisment for Nasmyth Wilson & Co. Ltd., showing Patricoft Works

After James left the company it continued to prosper, making railway locomotives into the twentieth century under the name Nasmyth Wilson and Co. By 1888 the site on the western side of Green Lane had been completely developed and by 1913 workers' cottages on the east side of the site had been replaced by a new office block and workshops. There was also a branch railway giving the company direct access to the London and North Western Railway. During the First World War,

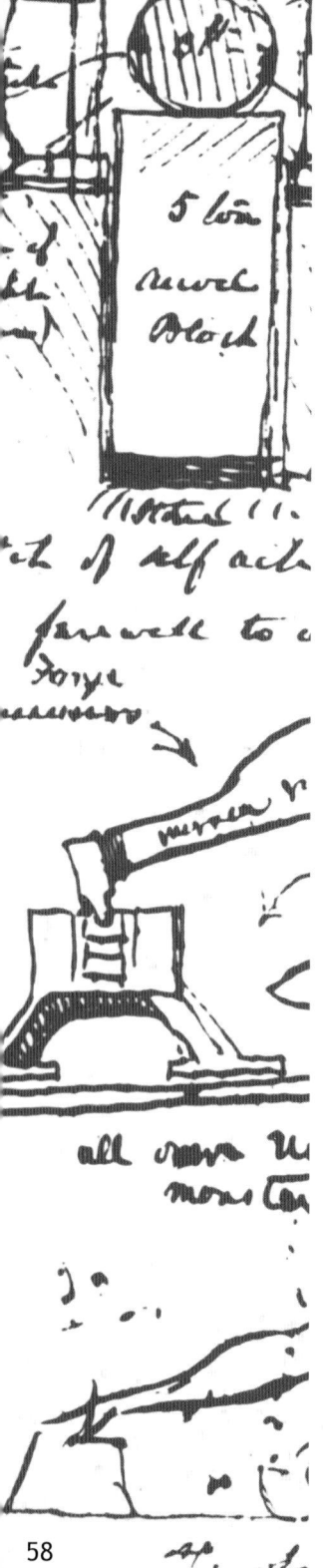

Nasmyth's played a full part in the war effort. In 1917 they manufactured, to the order of the Minister for Munitions at the War Office, "100 Petrol-Electric Tractors" for use on the French military railways. In 1922 the records show that 6 locomotives were built for use in Takoradi harbour on the Gold Coast (now Ghana) in West Africa at a cost of £7,725 each and which produced a profit of only 3.3%; times were becoming increasingly difficult for relatively small firms such as Nasmyths. In 1938, just about one hundred years after Nasmyths got their first order for a locomotive, two 2-6-4 type tank engines were the last to leave the works. Keeping up the tradition of building for export to the end, they were built for the South Indian Railways.

On June 1st 1940 the works were taken over by the Ministry of Supply and converted into a Royal Ordnance Factory. In April 1987 the Royal Ordnance factory was bought from the government by British Aerospace and so it remained until the end of the Cold War, when it finally closed in 1989.

The only monument to this great nineteenth-century engineer, apart from the one he designed himself in Dean Cemetry, Edinburgh, is a bronze plaque erected at number 47 York Place in Edinburgh, to mark his birthplace. In the Manchester area there is not even a public house called after him. There are, however, one or two Nasmyth machines still remaining in the district. A steam hammer stands outside one of the buildings of Bolton University and another, rescued by local people from the British Coal Board works at Elsecar in South Yorkshire, now guards the gate of an Industrial Park opposite Nasmyth's old works on Green Lane in Patricroft. The old factory buildings have been partly demolished and the remains are in poor repair and divided up into small workshops.

Samuel Smiles who edited Nasmyth's Autobiography said, "When I enquired of him for information in 1863 regarding his mechanical inventions he said 'my life presents no striking or remarkable incidents and would I fear prove but a tame narrative as the sphere to which my endeavours have been directed has been of a comparatively quiet order but vanity apart I hope I have been able to leave a few marks of my existence behind me in the shape of useful contrivances which are in many ways helping great works of industry.'" The reader must make up his own mind as to the success of Nasmyth's aspirations.

chapter 10

References & further reading

1. "The Bridgewater Foundry 1836 -1940" - John A. Cantrell - British Association for Local History 2004.

2. "James Nasmyth" - Raymond S Booth - City of Salford Educational Project - undated.

3. "Two Maudslay Proteges, Francis Lewis and George Nasmyth" - John A Cantrell - Trans. Newcomen Soc.73 2003

4. "James Nasmyth" - Audrey E Lumb - Eccles Library 1958.

5. "James Nasmyth Engineer"- Autobiography - Ed. Samuel Smiles 1883.

6. "James Nasmyth and the Bridgewater Foundry" - John A Cantrell - M/C University Press for Chetham Soc. Vol XXI, 1984.

7. Manuscript notes - F Mullineux

8. Unpublished notes - John A Cantrell. 2006.

9. Nasmyth, Wilson & Co. Patricroft Locomotive Builders" 2005.

10. "Industrial Biography" Samuel Smiles 1863.

11. "Alexander Nasmyth 1758 - 1840" J C B Cooksey, Paul Harris 1991

12. Talking About Nasmyth - Miss M Patry - Presidential Lecture to Eccles Hist. Soc.1971.

© *John Aldred, Worsley, 2008*

Notice

The Eccles and District History Society is proud to publish John Aldred's account of the life of James Nasmyth. Such an account has long been needed to make known the life and achievements of one of the most famous engineers of his time who also made contributions to astronomy and the arts.

It is the latest publication by the Society undertaken since its foundation on 1st February, 1956, to promote the study of local history. The following publications are available for purchase:

The Duke of Bridgewater's Canal, F. Mullineux £1.50 (80p p & p)

Golden Jubilee Miscellany of past lectures £3.00 (£2 p & p)

The Demise of Several Centuries of Basket Making in the Lower Irwell Valley £1.50 (£1 p & p)

Sets of many of the lectures given to the Society from 1970/71 to 1999/2002 are also on sale (£3.00, £2.00 p & p).

The Society promotes the study of local history in other ways. Each year it offers the Frank Mullineux Local History Award for work in local history. In 2007, with the help of a grant from the Heritage Lottery Fund, it began a programme for photographing local scenes and digitising local collections of photographs. Monthly talks and excursions are arranged and members receive the Society's Newsletter. For further information on the Society its website www.edhs.colsal.org.uk can be consulted and enquiries are welcome.

The Society gratefully acknowledges the receipt of a grant of £1,000 from Eccles Community Committee towards the publication of this book.